Nihil Obstat
Ecclesiastical Approbation

Montreal, Canada
July 5th, 1993

Nothing contrary to Catholic teaching.

'PEACE BE WITH YOU'

The Most Holy Face of Jesus. What a tremendous gift given to us by our Heavenly Father. Happy are those who hear His message. Happier and more blessed indeed are those who act upon it.

This little book is dedicated in total simplicity and trust to our precious Mother, Mary. May it be used to help souls love, console and make reparation to Jesus crucified.

This book is also dedicated in loving memory of Germaine Deery, a true apostle of the Holy Face of Jesus.

HOLY FACE ASSOCIATION
P. O. Box 1000, Station "A"
Montreal, Quebec, Canada
H3C 2W9

The Shroud (13 ft. by 3½ ft.) **as actually seen by the naked eye**
*Also showing the lozenge shaped mending patches and
the two figures, head to head*

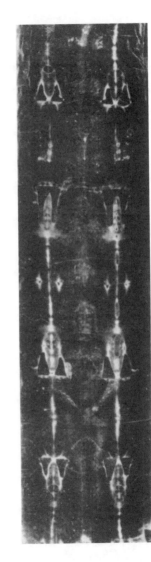

The full-length Shroud, showing the two figures head to head
As seen on the photographic negative

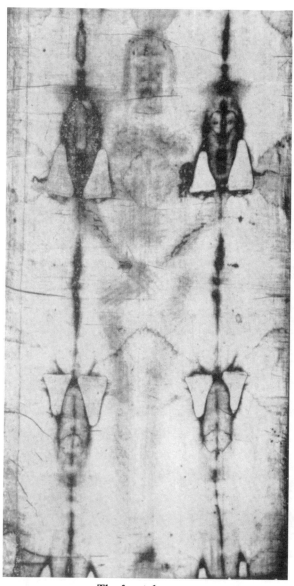

The frontal aspect
as seen in its actual state by the naked eye

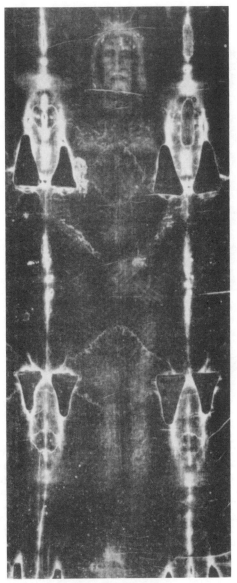

The frontal aspect
as seen on the photographic negative

"I desire that My Face which shows My Soul's deepest anguish, My Heart's sorrow and love, may be more honoured. Whoever gazes upon Me already consoles Me. Every time that anyone gazes at My Face, I will pour My love into hearts and by means of My Holy Face, the salvation of many souls will be obtained." *(Our Lord Jesus Christ to Sister Pierina)*

Table of Contents

Section IV - Holy Face Programs

Section I:
True Devotion to the Holy Face
Introduction

God loved the world so much that He gave His only Son, that everyone who has faith in Him may not die but have eternal life. It was not to judge the world that God sent His Son into the world but that through Him the world might be saved.

The man who puts his faith in Him does not come under judgement but the unbeliever has already been judged in that he has not given his allegiance to God's only Son. Here lies the test: the light has come into the world but man preferred darkness to light because their deeds were evil. Bad men all hate the light and avoid it for fear that their practices should be shown up. The honest man comes to the light so that it may be clearly seen that God is in all that he does. (John 3: 16-21)

Our Lord said, "When I return, will there be faith on earth?" We have been given an awesome opportunity by our Heavenly Father, the Devotion to the Most Holy Face of Jesus, His Most Beloved Son with Whom He was so well pleased. When someone is sick, they look for the remedy so that they may be cured. These are the days of Divine Love and Divine Mercy. We have been given a remedy for our days in which there is such a great lack of faith. We have been shown through a holy nun, Mother Pierina, how we can receive this great gift of faith and fortitude' as well as other important graces.

Our Lord did not make it difficult to do so. He has made this message for simple souls; "unless you become like a little child, you cannot enter into the kingdom of Heaven."

1

Please read this book like a little child, with the love and trust of a child in He who died for you and is now pleading for you to love and console Him. Won't you please ask your Guardian Angel to help you. He is always at your side, _ _ _ waiting.

To promote this devotion, the Holy Face Association was established in Montreal on May 26, 1976. The goal of this apostolate is reparation to God (Father, Son and Holy Spirit) through contemplative devotion to the Holy Face. This is accomplished through the diffusion of Holy Face pictures, leaflets and medals throughout the world. The apostolate recalls the words of St. Paul *"that Christ Crucified must be preached"*. This is not one more or less devotion; it is a plea from God.

MAY THE LORD BLESS YOU AND KEEP YOU.

MAY THE LORD LET HIS FACE SHINE ON YOU AND BE GRACIOUS TO YOU.

MAY THE LORD UNCOVER HIS FACE TO YOU AND BRING YOU PEACE.

"This is how they are to call down my name on the sons of Israel, and I will bless them." (Num. 6:22-27)

Gordon Deery, Servant

The Devotion to the Holy Face
as revealed to Sister Maria Pierina

GIUSEPPINA DE MICHELI was clothed with the habit of the Daughters of the Immaculate Conception on the 16th of May, 1916 and took the name of Sister Maria Pierina. A soul burning with love for Christ, she gave herself up unconditionally to her Divine Spouse Who, in turn, made her the object of His particular complacency. From her childhood, she nourished a desire for reparation which grew with her growth until it ended in a complete immolation of self. It is not surprising then that at the age of twelve, when she was in her Parochial Church (St. Peter in Sala, Milan) on Good Friday, she heard a voice saying quite distinctly: *"Nobody gives me a kiss of love in My Face to make amends for the Kiss of Judas."* In her childlike simplicity, she believed that the voice was heard by all and was pained to see that only the wounds were kissed but not the face. In her heart exclaiming, "Have patience, dear Jesus, I will give you a kiss of love", she imprinted a kiss on the Face will full ardour.

As a novice, she was permitted to do night adoration and on the night between Holy Thursday and Good Friday, while she was praying before the Crucifix, she heard it say *"Kiss Me"*. Sister Maria Pierina obeyed and her lips felt not the contact with the image of plaster but the contact of the true Face of Jesus. When her Mother Superior called her, it was morning and her heart was full of the sufferings of Jesus and of the desire to repair the outrages the Holy Face received and is daily receiving in the Most Holy Sacrament.

3

In 1919, Sister Maria Pierina was sent to the Mother House at Buenos Aires and on the 12th of April, 1920, when she was complaining to Jesus of one of her sorrows, He appeared to her bathed in blood and with a sorrowful and affectionate expression ("which I shall never forget", she writes), telling her *"What have I done?"*. Sister Maria Pierina understood and from that time the Holy Face of Jesus became to her a book for meditation and the entrance to His Heart. She returned to Milan in 1921 and Jesus continued to be her object of love. A little later, when she was elected Superior of the house of Milan and provincial for Italy, besides being the mother, she became the apostle of the Holy Face to the Sisters under her care and to all those with whom she came in contact. Mother Pierina knew how to hide everything and the Community is the only witness of certain facts. She asked Jesus the permission to conceal and it was granted her. As years passed, Jesus showed Himself to her often, sad and bleeding, asking her for reparation, thus increasing in her the desire to suffer and to immolate herself for the salvation of souls.

During the night adoration of the First Friday in Lent in 1936, Jesus after having made her participate in the mental sorrow of the agony in the Garden of Gethsemani, with His Face covered with blood and profoundly sad told her: *"I wish that My Face, which reflects the deep pains of My Soul, the sorrow and love of My Heart, be better honoured.   Who contemplates Me consoles Me."*

On the Tuesday following Passion Sunday, Jesus returned to her and said, *"every time My Face is contemplated, I will pour out My love into the heart of those persons and by the means of My*

Holy Face, the salvation of many souls will be obtained."

On the First Tuesday of 1937, while she was at prayer "after having instructed me on the devotion to His Holy Face" - she writes - He told me: *"Perhaps some souls fear that the devotion to My Holy Face will diminish that to My Heart. On the contrary, it will be a completion and augmentation of that devotion. Souls contemplating My Face participate in My Sorrow. They feel the necessity of love and reparation. Is not this the true devotion to My Heart?"*

These manifestations became more and more frequent and in May of 1938, while at prayer on the step of the Altar, a beautiful Lady appeared to her carrying in her hand a Scapular, made of two pieces of flannel, joined by a cord. One of these pieces bore the image of the Holy Face of Jesus with the words *"Let Thy Face shine upon us, O Lord"* and the other a Host surrounded by rays and the words *"Remain with us, Lord"*. Gently, the Lady approached her and said: *"Listen carefully and report everything to the Father. This scapular is an armour of defence, a shield of strength, a token of the love and mercy which Jesus wishes to give the world in these times of lust and hatred against God and His Church. Diabolical nets are thrown to wrench the Faith from hearts, evils abound, true apostles are few, and the remedy is the Holy Face of Jesus. All who wear a Scapular like this and make, if possible, every Tuesday a visit to the Blessed Sacrament, in order to repair the outrages which the Face of my Son Jesus received during His Passion and receives every day in the Holy Eucharist, will be strengthened in Faith,*

prompt to defend it

and to overcome all difficulties internal and external.

Further, they will have a peaceful death under the loving gaze of my Divine Son."

The request of Our Lady was increasingly pressing - but, Mother Pierina replied that it was not in her power to put it into execution. The permission of the one who guided her spiritual life and funds was necessary. The same year, Jesus appeared again, covered with blood, and with much sadness said, *"See how I suffer. Nevertheless, I am understood by so few. What ingratitude on the part of those who say they love Me. I have given My Heart as a sensible object of My great love for man and I give My Face as a sensible object of My Sorrow for the sins of man. I desire that it be honoured by a special feast on Tuesday in Quinquagesima (Shrove Tuesday - the Tuesday before Ash Wednesday). The feast will be preceded by a novena in which the faithful make reparation with Me uniting themselves with My Sorrow."*

In 1939, Jesus said again: *"I wish that My Holy Face be honoured in a particular manner on Tuesdays."* Mother Pierina felt the desire of Our Blessed Lady, manifested to her, very pressing. She obtained permission from her spiritual director. Though means were wanting, she set about the task. She obtained the permission of the photographer Bruner to take copies of the Holy Shroud as reproduced by him, and also the permission of the venerable Curia of Milan on the 9th of August, 1940. Financial means were still wanting, but the confidence of the Reverend

Mother made up for it. One morning, she saw on a little table an envelope. She opened it to find 11.200 Lire. Our Blessed Lady had seen to it.

The devil, maddened at this, fell upon this soul to frighten it and prevent the distribution of the medals. He threw her down in the corridor and down the steps; he tore the images and pictures of the Holy Face but she bore up everything. She tolerated and sacrificed all in order that thus the Holy Face may be honoured. She was worried because she got medals made instead of scapulars. She turned to Our Blessed Lady to obtain peace of mind in the matter. On the 17th of April, 1943, the Blessed Virgin appeared to her and said: *"My daughter, be calm. The scapulars have been substituted by the medal with the same promises and favours - it only remains to be distributed widely. Just now my heart is set on the feast of the Face of My Divine Son. Tell the Pope that it preoccupies me."* She blessed her and departed.

At present, the medal is spread with enthusiasm. What wonderful graces are being obtained, dangers averted, cures, conversions, the condemned liberated. How many, O how many!

On the 26th of July, 1945, Mother Pierina joined the One Whom she loved. Hers cannot be said to be death, but a transport of love. As she herself wrote in her diary on the 19th of July, 1941: "I feel a deep longing to live always united to Jesus and to love Him intensely because my death can only be a transport of love with my Spouse, Jesus."

INVOCATION

*My heart has said of you, "Seek His Face."
Yahweh, I do seek your face; do not hide your
face from me.* (Psalm 26, 8-9)

O Holy Face of my sweet Jesus, by that
tenderness of love and unspeakable grief with
which the Blessed Virgin Mary beheld Thee in Thy
painful Passion, grant that our souls may share in
that great love and great sorrow, and fulfill more
perfectly the Holy Will of God. Amen.

In 1940, when the Second World War had the
world in a turmoil, Italy saw a wide distribution of
this medal. Relatives and friends saw that their
soldiers, sailors, and aviators were provided with
the replica of the Holy Face since the medal was
already famous for its miracles and countless
spiritual and temporal favours.

The very first medal of the Holy Face was offered
to our glorious Pontiff, Pope Pius XII; then the
whole world got acquainted with this special
object of favours and devotion. It is to be found
on land and sea. Never has it been heard that a
prisoner of war wearing this badge of salvation
has been executed.

Our Lord wants this devotion to spread. He gives
wonderful graces and asks in return practically
nothing. What is asked of us, as revealed by our
Blessed Lady, is the sanctification of Tuesday by
making visits of reparation to Jesus in the Blessed
Sacrament. We should make expiation for our
own sins and the sins of others, who dishonour the
Sacred Face of Jesus by their ingratitude and
sinful lives. We should make it a point of
spreading this devotion. It is an easy means of

obtaining the salvation of sinners and our own as well.

Mother Maria Pierina De Micheli

O God, One in three Persons, Father, Son and Holy Spirit, you were pleased to let the gifts of your grace shine in the humble soul of Mother Pierina, and called her to your service in a hidden life of obedience to be consoler of the Crucified Jesus and missioner of His Holy Face. Grant us that we, too, may dedicate our whole life to the glory of Your Name and the service of our brothers and sisters.

Through the merits and intercession of your faithful servant, grant us also the favours we confidently ask, so that she may one day be honoured on your altars and her heroic virtues be shown forth for our example and encouragement. Amen.

Our Lord to Mother Pierina:

"By My Holy Face, you will obtain the conversion of numberless sinners. Nothing that you ask in making this offering will be refused

you. According to the care you take in making reparation to My Face, disfigured by blasphemers, I will take care of yours, which has been disfigured by sin. I will reprint upon it My Image, and render it as beautiful as it was on leaving the Baptismal Font. I promise personal and spiritual protection to all who venerate this medal."

"My beloved, to thee I renew the offering of My Face in order that you may offer it without ceasing to the Eternal Father. With this offering, you will obtain the salvation and sanctification of many souls. When, however, you will offer it through my priests, miracles will be worked." (May 23, 1938)

"Contemplate My Face and you will enter into My Heart's abyss of sorrow. Console Me and search for souls who sacrifice themselves with Me for the salvation of the world." (May 27, 1938)

On November 21, 1938, Our Lord appeared to Mother Pierina while she was doing a night of adoration. He was bleeding and said very sadly to her:

"Do you see how I suffer? Yet, very few understand me. Those who say they love me are very ungrateful. I have given my heart as the sensible object of my love to all, and I give My Face as the sensible object of my sorrow for the sins of the world. I wish that it be venerated by a special feast on Shrove Tuesday, (the day before Ash Wednesday),

preceded by a novena in which all the faithful make reparation with me, uniting themselves in participating with me in my sorrow."

"Rejoice, My Daughter, because the hour approaches when the most beautiful work under the sun will be born." - Our Lord refers here to the work of reparation to the Holy Face, which He revealed is destined to be the means of defeating atheistic Communism and restoring peace to the world. (To Sister Maria de St. Pierre)

Our Lord also said to Mother Pierina:

"Now, if there will still be those who will not recognize that this is truly My work, it is because they close their eyes." He also said *"you will know my disciples by their works"*, so we ask you to please persevere in helping others to know of this devotion of love and mercy.

Pope Pius IX said: "THIS SALUTARY REPARATION TO THE HOLY FACE OF JESUS IS A DIVINE WORK, DESTINED TO SAVE MODERN SOCIETY."

St. Pius X expressed the desire that it be venerated in the homes of all Christian families.

Pope Pius XI gave pictures of the Holy Face from the Shroud to youths saying, "They are pictures of the Divine Son of Mary; they come, in fact, from that object known as the Shroud of Turin; still mysterious, but certainly not the work of any human hand."

Pope Pius XII asked to spread knowledge and veneration of so great and sacred a relic.

Pope John XXIII, on seeing the relic, said, "This can only be the Lord's own doing."

Pope Paul VI praised the Holy Shroud saying "Perhaps only the Image from the Holy Shroud reveals to us something of the human and divine personality of Christ."

Pope John Paul II, after kissing the Holy Shroud with the accompanying Bishops, referred to the Holy Shroud as a "silent but amazingly eloquent witness of the resurrection of Christ."

Many popes have placed special blessings on those who venerate the Most Holy Face of Jesus, some even stating that these blessings are never to be taken away.

St. Ambrose states: "There is no doubt that Peter received the grace of conversion from the Sacred Face because those on whom Jesus gazes are always saved."

St. Jerome: "The Face of Jesus will continue to save each time we have recourse to it; invoking His aid, "Show us Thy Face and we shall be saved."

Other Saints, who have venerated the Holy Face, to mention a few, are: St. Gregory the Great, St.

Gertrude the Great, St. John Chrysostum, St. Ambrose, St. Bernard, St. Charles Borromeo, St. John Bosco, St. Francis of Assisi, St. Catherine of Sienna, St. Augustine, and, of course, St. Theresa of the Child Jesus and the Holy Face.

St. Theresa of Lisieux commented: "How much good the Holy Face has done me during my life. The Holy Face was a continual call to her to suffer so that she might resemble Jesus." St. Theresa says, "The just will recognize Him not only by the cross - symbol of salvation, which will precede His coming, but more exactly, by His Face, which will shine on the last day."

Surely it was not without reason that God permitted us to have this great honor. Evidently, Our Lord's intention is to turn our thoughts with special tenderness and love towards the sufferings of His adorable Face.

The Feast of the Holy Face of Jesus

On April 17, 1958, His Holiness Pope Pius XII confirmed the Feast of the Holy Face of Jesus on Shrove Tuesday (Tuesday before Ash Wednesday), for ALL THE DIOCESES AND RELIGIOUS ORDERS who would ask for the Indult from Rome in order to celebrate it.

"All those who, attracted by my love, and venerating my countenance, shall receive, by virtue of my humanity, a brilliant and vivid impression of my divinity. This splendour shall enlighten the depths of their souls, so that in

eternal glory the celestial court shall marvel at the marked likeness of their features with my divine countenance." (Our Lord Jesus Christ to St. Gertrude)

If you are not able to get to a church, then you are advised to venerate the Most Holy Face of Jesus in your home.

To receive Holy Face Medal, please send self-addressed, double- stamped envelope to:

HOLY FACE ASSOCIATION
P. O. Box 1000, Station "A"
Montreal, Quebec, Canada
H3C 2W9

NINE DAY NOVENA
in HONOUR of and REPARATION to
the HOLY FACE of JESUS

PRAYER TO SAINT MICHAEL

St. Michael, the Archangel, defend us in this day of Battle; Be our safeguard against the wickedness and snares of the devil. May God rebuke him, we humbly pray, and do Thou, O Prince of the Heavenly Host, by the power of God, cast into hell, Satan and all the other evil spirits, who prowl throughout the world, seeking the ruin of souls. Amen.

PRAYER TO THE HOLY SPIRIT

O, Holy Spirit, in these days of doubt, confusion, and uncertainty, come into our hearts with your light, your strength and your consolation. Come with the light of truth and teach us the will of God in our daily living, especially now when God's basic laws are challenged or ignored.

Come with your strength that purifies our heart and our desires and guards us against the danger of pride and self-conceit. Bring your consolation so that with a heart attuned to your holy love, we may live in peace and harmony in our families and give to our communities the spirit of cooperation, tolerance and understanding.

O God, you have instructed the faithful with the light of the Holy Spirit. Grant that through this same Holy Spirit we may be truly wise and enjoy His consolation always. Amen.

DAILY PREPARATORY PRAYER

O Most Holy and Blessed Trinity, through the intercession of Holy Mary, whose soul was pierced through by a sword of sorrow at the sight of the passion of her Divine Son, we ask your help in making a perfect Novena of reparation with Jesus, united with all His sorrows, love, and total abandonment. We now implore all the Angels and Saints to intercede for us as we pray this Holy Novena to the Most Holy Face of Jesus and for the glory of the most Holy Trinity, Father, Son, and Holy Spirit. Amen. (Start novena)

FIRST DAY

(Console Holy Face and recite Daily Preparatory Prayer on page 16)

Psalm 51, 3-4:

Have mercy on me, O God in your goodness,

in your great tenderness wipe away my faults;

wash me clean of my guilt, purify me from my sin.

O Most Holy Face of Jesus, look with tenderness on us who are sinners. You are a merciful God, full of love and compassion. Keep us pure of heart so that we may see Thee always. Mary, our Mother, intercede for us; Saint Joseph, pray for us.

Through the merits of your precious blood and your Holy Face, O Jesus, grant us our petition,.............pardon and mercy.

PRAYER TO OUR ALMIGHTY FATHER

Almighty Father, come into our hearts, and so fill us with your love that forsaking all evil desires, we may embrace you, our only good. Show us, O Lord our God, what you are to us. Say to our souls, I am your salvation, speak so that we may hear. Our hearts are before you; open our ears; let us hasten after your voice. Hide not your Face from us, we beseech you, O Lord. Open our hearts so that you may enter in. Repair the ruined mansions, that you may dwell therein. Hear us, O Heavenly Father, for the sake of your only Son, Our Lord Jesus Christ, who lives and reigns with you and the Holy Spirit, one God, now and forever. Amen. (St. Augustine)

Pray one (1) Our Father, three (3) Hail Mary's and one (1) Glory Be.

"Oh Jesus, through the merits of your Holy Face, have pity on us, and on the whole world." *(Three times)*

SECOND DAY

(Console Holy Face and recite Daily Preparatory Prayer on page 16)

Psalm 51, Verse 2:

My offenses truly I know them;

My sin is always before me.

Against you, you alone, have I sinned;

What is evil in your sight I have done.

Most Holy Face of Jesus, we are truly sorry that we have hurt you so much by constantly doing what is wrong; and for all the good works that we have failed to do. Immaculate Heart of Mary, Saint Joseph, intercede for us, help us to console the Most Holy Face of Jesus. Pray that we may share in the tremendous love You have for one another, and for the Most Blessed Trinity. Amen.

Through the merits of your precious blood and your Holy Face, O Jesus, grant us our petition,............. pardon and mercy.

PRAYER TO THE HOLY SPIRIT

Come, Holy Spirit, Sanctifier, all powerful God of love, Thou who didst fill the Virgin Mary with grace, Thou who didst wonderfully transform the hearts of the apostles, Thou who didst endow all Thy martyrs with a miraculous heroism, come and sanctify us, illumine our minds, strengthen our wills, purify our consciences, rectify our judgments, set our hearts on fire and preserve us from the misfortune of resisting Thy inspirations. We consecrate to Thee our understanding, our heart and our will, our whole being for time and for eternity. May our understanding be always submissive to Thy heavenly inspirations and to the teachings of Thy Holy Catholic Church, of which Thou art the infallible guide; may our heart be ever inflamed with love of God and neighbor; may our will be ever conformed to the divine will, and may our whole life be a faithful imitation of the life and virtues of our Lord and Saviour, Jesus Christ, to whom with the Father and Thee be honor and glory forever. Amen.

Pray one (1) Our Father, three (3) Hail Mary's and one (1) Glory Be.

"Oh Jesus, through the merits of your Holy Face, have pity on us, and on the whole world." *(Three times)*

THIRD DAY

(Console Holy Face and recite Daily Preparatory Prayer on page 16)

Psalm 51, Verse 3:

You are just when you pass sentence on me,

blameless when you give judgement

You know I was born guilty,

a sinner from the moment of conception.

PRAYER OF POPE PIUS IX

O Jesus! Cast upon us a look of mercy; turn your Face towards each of us as you did Veronica; not that we may see it with our bodily eyes, for this we do not deserve, but turn it towards our hearts, so that, remembering you, we may ever draw from this fountain of strength the vigor necessary to sustain the combats of life. Amen. Mary, our Mother, and Saint Joseph, pray for us.

Through the merits of your precious blood and your Holy Face, O Jesus, grant us our petition,............ pardon and mercy.

PRAYER OF SAINT FRANCIS

All highest, glorious God, cast your light into the darkness of our hearts, give us true faith, firm hope, perfect charity and profound humility, so that with wisdom, courage and perception, O Lord, we may do what is truly your holy will. Amen.

(continued...)

TO THE ANGELS AND SAINTS

We salute you, through the Holy Face and sacred Heart of Jesus, O all you Holy Angels and Saints of God. We rejoice in your glory and we give thanks to our Lord for all the benefits which He has showered upon you; we praise Him, and glorify Him, and offer you for an increase of your joy and honor, the most Holy Face and gentle Heart of Jesus. Pray that we may become formed according to the heart of God. Amen.

Pray one (1) Our Father, three (3) Hail Mary's and one (1) Glory Be.

"Oh Jesus, through the merits of your Holy face, have pity on us, and on the whole world." *(Three times)*

FOURTH DAY

(Console Holy Face and recite Daily Preparatory Prayer on page 16)

Psalm 51, Verse 4:

Indeed you love truth in the heart;

then in the secret of my heart teach me wisdom.

O purify me, then I shall be clean;

O wash me, I shall be whiter than snow.

O Lord Jesus, who has said, learn of me for I am meek and gentle of heart, and who did manifest upon Thy Holy Face the sentiments of Thy divine heart, grant that we may love to come frequently and meditate upon Thy divine features. We may read there thy gentleness and Thy humility, and learn how to form our hearts in the practice of these two virtues which Thou desires to see shine in Thy servants. Mary, our Mother, and Saint Joseph, help us.

Through the merits of Thy precious blood and your Holy Face, O Jesus, grant us our petition,............., pardon and mercy.

PRAYER IN HONOR OF THE DOLORS OF THE BLESSED VIRGIN MARY

O Most Holy and afflicted Virgin, Queen of Martyrs! Who stood beneath the cross, witnessing the agony of your dying Son, look down with a mother's tenderness and pity on us as we kneel before you to venerate your Dolors and place our requests, with filial confidence, in the sanctuary of your wounded heart. Present them on our behalf to Jesus, through the merits of His most Sacred Passion and Death, together with your sufferings at the foot of the cross, and through the united efficacy of both, obtain the favor which we humbly ask. To whom shall we go in our wants and miseries if not to you? O Mother of Mercy, who having so deeply drunk of the chalice of your Son, graciously alleviate the sufferings of those who still sigh in this land of exile. Amen.

PRAYER FOR THE SOULS IN PURGATORY

My Jesus, by the sorrows you suffered in your agony in the garden, in your scourging and crowning with thorns, in the way to Calvary, in your crucifixion and death, have mercy on the souls in Purgatory, and especially on those that are most forsaken. Deliver them from the dire torments which they endure. Call them and admit them to your most sweet embrace in Paradise. Amen.

Pray one (1) Our Father, three (3) Hail Mary's and one (1) Glory Be.

"Oh Jesus, through the merits of your Holy Face, have pity on us, and on the whole world." *(Three times)*

FIFTH DAY

(Console Holy face and recite Daily Preparatory Prayer on page 16)

Psalm 51, Verse 5:

Make me hear rejoicing and gladness,

that the bones you have crushed may revive.

From my sins turn away your Face,

and blot out all my guilt.

Holy Face of Jesus, Sacred Countenance of God, how great is your patience with humankind, how infinite your forgiveness. We are sinners, yet you love us. This gives us courage. For the glory of your Holy Face and of the Blessed Trinity, hear and answer us. Mary our Mother, intercede for us, Saint Joseph, pray for us.

Through the merits of your pecious blood and your Holy Face, O Jesus, grant us our petition,..............., pardon and mercy.

PRAYER TO SAINT JOSEPH

Dear Saint Joseph! Adopt us as thy children, take charge of our salvation; watch over us day and night; preserve us from occasions of sin; obtain for us purity of body and soul, and the spirit of prayer, through thy intercession with Jesus, grant us a spirit of sacrifice, of humility and self-denial; obtain for us a burning love for Jesus in the Blessed Sacrament, and a sweet, tender love for

Mary, our Mother. Saint Joseph, be with us in life, be with us in death, and obtain for us a favourable judgement from Jesus, our merciful Saviour. Amen.

Pray one (1) Our Father, three (3) Hail Mary's and one (1) Glory Be.

"Oh Jesus, through the merits of your Holy Face, have pity on us, and on the whole world." *(Three times)*

SIXTH DAY

(Console Holy Face and recite Daily Preparatory Prayer on page 16)

Psalm 51, Verse 6:

A pure heart create for us O God,

put a steadfast spirit within us.

Do not cast us away from your presence

nor deprive us of your Holy Spirit.

May our hearts be cleansed, O Lord, by the inpouring of the Holy Spirit, and may He render them fruitful by watering them with His heavenly dew. Mary, the most chaste spouse of the Holy Spirit, intercede for us, Saint Joseph pray for us.

Through the merits of your precious blood and your Holy Face, O Jesus, grant us our petition,............, pardon and mercy.

PRAYER TO SAINT MICHAEL THE ARCHANGEL

O Victorious Prince, most humble guardian of the Church of God and of faithful souls, who with such charity and zeal took part in so many conflicts and gained such great victories over the enemy, for the conservation and protection of the honor and glory we all owe to God, as well as for the promotion of our salvation; come, we pray Thee, to our assistance, for we are continually besieged with such great perils by our enemies, the flesh, the world, and the devil; and as Thou wert a leader for the people of God through the desert, so also be our faithful leader and companion through the desert of this world, until Thou conduct us safely into the happy land of the living, in that blessed fatherland from which we are all exiles. Amen.

(St. Aloysius)

Pray one (1) Our Father, three (3) Hail Mary's and one (1) Glory Be.

"Oh Jesus, through the merits of your Holy Face, have pity on us, and on the whole world." *(Three times)*

SEVENTH DAY

(Console Holy Face and recite Daily Preparatory Prayer on page 16)

Psalm 51, Verse 7:

Give me again the joy of your help,

with a spirit of fervor sustain me,

that I may teach transgressors your ways

and sinners may return to you.

Lord Jesus! After contemplating Thy features, disfigured by grief, after meditating upon Thy passion with compunction and love, how can our hearts fail to be inflamed with a holy hatred of sin, which even now outrages Thy Adorable Face! Lord, suffer us not to be content with mere compassion, but give us grace so closely to follow Thee in this calvary, so that the opprobrium destined for Thee may fall on us, O Jesus, that thus we may have a share, small though it may be, in expiation of sin. Amen. Mary, our Mother, intercede for us, Saint Joseph, pray for us.

Through the merits of your precious blood and your Holy Face, O Jesus, grant us our petition,............, pardon and mercy.

PRAYER IN HONOR OF MARY

Hail Mary, daughter of God the Father! Hail Mary, mother of God the Son! Hail Mary, spouse of the Holy Spirit! Hail Mary, temple of the Most Holy Trinity! Hail Mary, our mistress, our wealth, our mystic rose, Queen of our hearts, our Mother, our life, our sweetness and our dearest hope! We are all Thine, and all that we have is Thine. O Virgin blessed above all things, may Thy soul be in us to magnify the Lord; may Thy spirit be in us to rejoice in God. Place Thyself, O faithful Virgin, as a seal upon our hearts, that in Thee and through Thee we may be found faithful to God. Grant, most gracious Virgin, that we may be numbered among those whom Thou art pleased to love, to teach and to guide, to favor and to protect as Thy children. Grant that with the help of Thy love, we may despise all earthly consolation and cling to heavenly things, until through the Holy Spirit, Thy faithful spouse, and through Thee, His faithful spouse, Jesus Christ, Thy Son, be formed within us for the glory of the Father. Amen. (St. Grignon de Montfort)

Pray one (1) Our Father, three (3) Hail Mary's and one (1) Glory Be.

"Oh Jesus, through the merits of your Holy Face, have pity on us, and on the whole world." *(Three times)*

EIGHTH DAY

(Console Holy Face and recite Daily Preparatory Prayer on page 16)

Psalm 51, Verse 8:

O rescue me, God my helper,

and my tongue shall ring out your goodness.

O Lord, open my lips,

and my mouth shall declare your praise.

Most merciful Face of Jesus, who in this vale of tears was so moved by our misfortunes to call yourself the healer of the sick, and the good Shepherd of the souls gone astray, allow not satan to draw us away from you, but keep us always under your loving protection, together with all souls who endeavor to console you.

Mary, our Mother, intercede for us, Saint Joseph, pray for us.

Through the merits of your precious blood and your Holy Face, O Jesus, grant us our petition,............, pardon and mercy.

PRAYER TO SAINT PETER

O glorious Saint Peter, who in return for thy lively and generous faith, thy profound and sincere humility and thy burning love, was honored by Jesus Christ with singular privileges, and in particular, with the leadership of the other apostles and the primacy of the whole Church, of which thou were made the foundation stone, do thou obtain for us the grace of a lively faith, that shall not fear to profess itself openly in its entirety and in all of its manifestations, even to the shedding of blood, if occasion should demand it, and to the sacrifice of life itself in preference to surrender. Obtain for us likewise a sincere loyalty to our Holy Mother, the Church. Grant that we may ever remain most closely and sincerely united to the Holy Father, who is the heir of thy faith and of thy authority, the one true visible head of the Catholic Church. Grant, moreover, that we may follow, in all humility and meekness, the Church's teaching and counsels and may be obedient to all her precepts, in order to be able here on earth to enjoy a peace that is sure and undisturbed, and to attain one day in Heaven to everlasting happiness. Amen.

Pray one (1) Our Father, three (3) Hail Mary's and one (1) Glory Be.

"Oh Jesus, through the merits of your Holy Face, have pity on us, and on the whole world." *(Three times)*

NINTH DAY

(Console Holy Face and recite Daily Preparatory Prayer on page 16)

Psalm 51, Verse 9:

For in sacrifice you take no delight,

burnt offering from me you would refuse,

my sacrifice a contrite spirit.

A humbled, contrite heart you will not spurn.

(continued...)

Psalm 51, Verse 10:

In your goodness, show favour to Zion;

rebuild the walls of Jerusalem.

Then you will be pleased with lawful sacrifice,

holocausts offered on your altar.

Sacred Face of our Lord and our God, what words can we say to express our gratitude? How can we speak of our joy? That you have deigned to hear us, that you have chosen to answer us in our hour of need. We say this because we know that our prayers will be granted. We know that you, in your loving kindness, listened to our pleading hearts, and will give, out of your fullness, the answer to our problems. Mary, our Mother, thank you for your intercession on our behalf. Saint Joseph, thank you for your prayers.

Through the merits of your precious blood and your Holy Face, O Jesus, grant us our petition,............, pardon and mercy.

PRAYER TO THE HOLY TRINITY

Most Holy Trinity, Godhead indivisible, Father, Son and Holy Spirit, our first beginning and our last end. Since you have made us after your own image and likeness, grant that all the thoughts of our minds, all the words of our tongues, all the affections of our hearts and all our actions may be always conformed to your most Holy Will, so that after having seen you here on earth in appearances and in a dark manner by the means of faith, we may come at last to contemplate you face to face, in the perfect possession of you forever in Paradise. Amen.

Pray one (1) Our Father, three (3) Hail Mary's and one (1) Glory Be.

"Oh Jesus, through the merits of your Holy Face, have pity on us, and on the whole world." *(Three times)*

Recite the following Act of Consecration:

ACT OF CONSECRATION

O Lord Jesus, we believe most firmly in You, we love You. You are the Eternal Son of God and the Son Incarnate of the Blessed Virgin Mary. You are the Lord and Absolute Ruler of all creation. We acknowledge You, therefore, as the Universal Sovereign of all creatures. You are the Lord and Supreme Ruler of all mankind, and we, in acknowledging this Your dominion, consecrate ourselves to You now and forever. Loving Jesus, we place our families under the protection of Your Holy Face, and of Your Virgin Mother, Mary most sorrowful. We promise to be faithful to You for the rest of our lives and to observe with fidelity Your Holy Commandments. We will never deny before the world, You and Your Divine rights over us and all humankind. Grant us the grace to never sin again; nevertheless, should we fail, O Divine Saviour, have mercy on us and restore us to Your grace. Radiate Your Divine Countenance upon us and bless us now and forever. Embrace us at the hour of death in Your Kingdom for all eternity, through the intercession of Your Blessed Mother, of all Your Saints who behold You in Heaven, and the just who glorify You on earth. O Jesus, be mindful of us forever and never forsake us; protect our families. O Mother of Sorrows, by the eternal glory which you enjoy in Heaven, through the merits of your bitter anguish in the Sacred

Passion of your Beloved Son, our Lord Jesus Christ, obtain for us the grace that the Precious Blood shed by Jesus for the redemption of our souls, be not shed for us in vain. We love you, O Mary. Embrace us and bless us, O Mother. Protect us in life and in death. Amen.

Glory be to the Father, and to the Son, and to the Holy Spirit. As it was in the beginning, is now, and will be forever. Amen.

Section II :
Holy Hour of Reparation

(For the Holy Sacrifice of the Mass, see p. 47)

Exposition of the Blessed Sacrament

O SALUTARIS HOSTIA

O Salutaris Hostia,

Quae coeli pandis ostium!

Bella premunt hostilia;

Da robur fer auxilium.

Uni Trinoque Domino,

Sit sempiterna gloria;

Qui vitam sine termino

Nobis donet in patria. Amen.

OPENING PRAYER

Adorable Face of Jesus, whom all the angels adore, may you be known, loved and adored by the whole world. Sacred Face of Jesus, we desire to love and honor you more and more in reparation during this Holy Hour for the many sins committed against you. Through the merits of your Precious Blood and your Holy Face, we beg your pardon and mercy.

RESPONSORIAL PSALM (Psalm 51)

Response (Psalm 80:3): "Lord, let the light of your face shine on us and we shall be saved."

Have mercy on me, O God, in your goodness,
in your great tenderness wipe away my faults;
wash me clean of my guilt,
purify me from my sin.   RESPONSE

Yet, since you love sincerity of heart,
teach me the secrets of wisdom.
Purify me with hyssop until I am clean;
wash me until I am whiter than snow.   RESPONSE

Instill some joy and gladness into me,
let the bones you have crushed rejoice again.
Hide your face from my sins,
wipe out all my guilt.   RESPONSE

O God, create a clean heart in me,
put into me a new and constant spirit,
do not banish me from your presence,
do not deprive me of your Holy Spirit.   RESPONSE

LITANY OF THE HOLY FACE

In the words of our Lord Jesus Christ to Sister Pierina, *"I firmly wish that my face reflecting the intimate pains of my soul, the suffering and love of my heart, be more honored! Whoever gazes upon me already consoles me."*

Lord, have mercy on us.

Christ, have mercy on us.

Lord have mercy on us.   Christ, hear us.

Christ, graciously hear us.
God, the Father in Heaven, *have mercy on us.*
God, the Son, Redeemer of the world,
                                                         have mercy on us.
God, the Holy Spirit, *have mercy on us.*
Holy Trinity, One God, *have mercy on us.*
Adorable Face of Jesus, masterpiece of
   the Holy Spirit, *save us.*
Adorable Face of Jesus, perfect image
   of the humanity of Mary, *save us.*
Adorable Face of Jesus, everlasting joy
   in the sight of Mary and Joseph, *save us.*
Adorable Face of Jesus, adored by the
   Angels in Bethlehem, *save us.*
Adorable Face of Jesus, Splendor of the
   Holy Family, *save us.*
Adorable Face of Jesus, vanquisher of
   demons, *save us.*
Adorable Face of Jesus, consoling
   relief of sinners, *save us.*
Adorable Face of Jesus, gentle relief of
   the burdened, *save us.*
Adorable Face of Jesus, affirmer of
   brotherly charity, *save us.*
Adorable Face of Jesus, shining like the
   sun on Mount Thabor, *save us.*
Adorable Face of Jesus, resplendent joy
   of the Apostles, *save us.*

Adorable Face of Jesus, bowed to the
ground in the Garden of Gethsemane, *save us.*
Adorable Face of Jesus, whose glance
caused Peter to weep bitterly, *save us.*
Adorable Face of Jesus, covered, struck
and taunted in the brutal buffeting, *save us.*
Adorable Face of Jesus, covered with
spittle from vile mouths, *save us.*
Adorable Face of Jesus, whose Head
was crowned with thorns and struck
with a reed, *save us.*
Adorable Face of Jesus, taunted in the
horrible agony, *save us.*
Adorable Face of Jesus, praying for Your
executioners, *save us.*
Adorable Face of Jesus, whose pitiable
sight grieved the Mother of Sorrows, *save us.*
Adorable Face of Jesus, veiled in the
pallor of death, *save us.*
Adorable Face of Jesus, imprinted on the
Holy Shroud, *save us.*
Adorable Face of Jesus, resplendent on
Easter Morning, *save us.*
Adorable Face of Jesus, radiant in the
Ascension, *save us.*
Adorable Face of Jesus, Splendor of
Paradise, *save us.*

Adorable Face of Jesus, adoration of
the Angels,   *save us.*

Adorable Face of Jesus, everlasting joy
of the Saints,   *save us.*

Adorable Face of Jesus, calling the Elect
to Eternal Glory,   *save us.*

Adorable Face of Jesus, veiled in the
Adorable Sacrament of the Altar,   *save us.*

Lamb of God, Who take away the sins
of the world,   *spare us, O Lord.*

Lamb of God, Who take away the sins
of the world,   *graciously hear us, O Lord.*

Lamb of God, Who take away the sins
of the world,   *have mercy on us.*

V. Lord, show us your Face,

R. And we shall be saved.

Let us pray: Eternal Father, through the
Immaculate Heart of Mary, we offer you the Holy
Face of Jesus. May we who meditate on the
countenance of your Son, be a consoling influence
in His body, the Church. May we profit from the
merits of His passion, death and resurrection.
And may we be found worthy to walk in the way of
the cross. Amen.

PRAYER of ST. THERESA of JESUS to THE HOLY FACE

O Jesus, who in Thy bitter Passion didst become
"the most abject of men, a man of sorrows", I
venerate Thy Sacred Face whereon there once

did shine the beauty and sweetness of the Godhead; but now it has become for me as if it were the face of a leper! Nevertheless, under those disfigured features, I recognize Thy infinite Love and I am consumed with the desire to love Thee and make Thee loved by all. The tears which well up abundantly in Thy sacred eyes appear to me as so many precious pearls that I love to gather up, in order to purchase the souls of poor sinners by means of their infinite value. O Jesus, whose adorable Face ravishes my heart, I implore Thee to fix deep within me Thy Divine Image and to set me on fire with Thy Love, that I may be found worthy to come to the contemplation of Thy glorious Face in Heaven. Amen.

PRAYER OF MOTHER MARIA-PIERINA

O Blessed Face of my kind Saviour, by the tender love and piercing sorrow of Our Lady as she beheld You in Your cruel Passion, grant us to share in this intense sorrow and love so as to fulfill the Holy will of God to the utmost of our ability. Amen.

PRAYER OF ELIZABETH OF THE TRINITY

O my God, Trinity whom I adore! Help me to become utterly forgetful of self, that I may bury myself in Thee, as changeless and as calm as though my soul were already in eternity. May nothing disturb my peace or draw me out of Thee, O my immutable Lord! But may I at every moment penetrate more deeply into the depths of Thy mystery! Give peace to my soul; make it Thy Heaven, Thy cherished dwelling place, Thy home of rest. Let me never leave Thee there alone, but keep me there, all absorbed in Thee, in living faith, adoring Thee and wholly yielded up to Thy creative action! Amen.

ACT OF REPARATION

Presider: Let us humbly offer an act of reparation to the Holy Face of Jesus for the sacrileges, outrages and indifferences by which He is offended.

All: We adore you and praise you, our Lord Jesus, Son of the living God. And we desire to make sacrifices for the sacrileges, outrages and indifferences by which you are offended. Particularly for those which we, ourselves have committed or caused towards you in the members of Your Blessed Body, the Church. Receive our tender sentiments which we promise to ratify by our actions and deeds.

Most Holy Trinity, Father, Son and Holy Spirit, we adore you profoundly (all bow). We offer you the most precious Body, Blood, Soul and Divinity of our Lord, Jesus Christ, present in all the tabernacles throughout the world, in reparation for all the sacrileges, outrages and indifferences by which He is offended. By the infinite merits of the Sacred Heart of Jesus, which are manifested in His Holy Face, and by the merits of the Immaculate Heart of Mary, we beg the conversion of poor sinners.

Presider: God, our Father, may You receive this offering through Christ, our Lord.

All: Amen.

The prayer of the Golden Arrow, in the words of Jesus to Mother St. Pierre, "is an act of praise of the Holy Name of God, which is the aim and purpose of this Sacred Devotion to the Holy and Crucified Face of Jesus, our Blessed Lord and Saviour."

THE GOLDEN ARROW

May the most holy, most sacred, most adorable, most incomprehensible and ineffable Name of God be forever praised, blessed, loved, adored and glorified in Heaven, on earth, and under the earth, by all the creatures of God, and by the Sacred Heart of Our Lord Jesus Christ, in the Most Holy Sacrament of the Altar. Amen. (Dictated by Our Lord to Sr. Marie of St. Peter)

Eternal Father, I offer Thee the adorable Face of Thy Beloved Son for the honor and glory of Thy Name, for the conversion of sinners and the salvation of the dying. Amen.

SERVICE OF ANOINTING

(May be done during or after the Holy Hour)

An anointing with the Oil of the Sacred and Holy Face of Jesus Crucified.

It is not necessary for a priest to give the anointing, as the oil has been blessed with an ordinary blessing. During the annointing (which should be done by making the sign of the Cross with oil on the forhead and both palms of each person), soft music should be played, with, if possible, adoration of the Blessed Sacrament and Holy Face of Jesus.

"Gracious and ever-loving Father, in the grace of the Divine Spirit, by the power of the Holy Name of Jesus, we beseech Thee to bless this oil of healing and goodness. May Mary, the Blessed Mother, Queen of all the angels and saints, intercede for all of us who seek mercy and forgiveness."

As each person comes to be signed and blessed, the following prayer will be said:

"May the Lord bless and keep you. May the light of His Holy Face protect you and give you His peace. May the Lord heal you in both mind and body."

And each person answers: *"May the Holy Name of Jesus be forever praised. Amen."*

All: *"O Lord, let the light of Your Face shine upon us and we shall be saved."* (To be said three times)

HOMILY, TESTIMONIALS and ROSARY RECITATION

THE JOYFUL MYSTERIES

1. THE ANNUNCIATION was a direction to Mary by the Angel Gabriel, asking her consent to become God's Mother. Assured of the miraculous preservation of her sacred Virginity, she freely and fully gave herself to God. *Ask her to give you the gift of a strong faith.*

2. THE VISITATION. At the sound of Mary's voice, John the Baptist was sanctified and Elizabeth, filled with the Holy Spirit, cried out: "Blessed art thou among women and blessed is the fruit of thy womb!" *Ask for the grace to bring Christ to your brothers and sisters.*

3. THE BIRTH OF JESUS IN BETHLEHEM'S STABLE came about because there was no room for Mary and Joseph at the inn. Shepherds sent by an Angel and wise men illuminated by a star came to adore Him. *Ask God's Mother to share in the love of the Holy Family*

4. THE PRESENTATION OF JESUS IN THE TEMPLE took place on the fortieth day after His birth. Simeon foretold Christ's final rejection and Mary's share in the crucifixion. *Ask for the spirit of self-sacrifice for the conversion of poor sinners.*

5. THE FINDING OF JESUS IN THE TEMPLE took place when He was twelve. Mary and Joseph sought Him for three days and finally found Him sitting among the doctors who were astounded by His wisdom. *Ask to find Jesus in every detail of your life.*

THE SORROWFUL MYSTERIES

1. THE AGONY OF JESUS IN THE GARDEN lasted three hours and caused Him to sweat blood at the sight of our sins and of the atrocious torments He was about to endure for them. Despite His human fear, He cried to His Father: "Not my will but thine

be done!" *Ask for true sorrow of your sins.*

2. THE SCOURGING AT THE PILLAR caused Jesus to be publically stripped and flogged from head to foot to atone for our sins, especially for those of the flesh. *Ask for the grace to practice Christian purity.*

3. THE CROWNING WITH THORNS - Jesus was mocked with a helmet of sharp thorns which was beaten down upon His head in derision of His kingship to atone for our pride and for our sins of thought. *Ask for the grace to learn of Him to be meek and humble of heart.*

4. THE CARRYING OF THE CROSS - Jesus is forced to carry the cross on His lacerated shoulders through the streets of Jerusalem. *Ask for the grace to bear each day's difficulties with patience, in union with Jesus.*

5. THE CRUCIFIXION - On Good Friday, Jesus was nailed hands and feet to the cross and hung there for three hours in untold mortal agony - for our sins. After His death, His Heart was pierced with a lance. *"Into Thy Hands I commend My spirit."*

THE GLORIOUS MYSTERIES

1. THE RESURRECTION - Christ rose from the tomb glorious and immortal on Easter morning, still bearing in His hands, feet and side the marks of His wounds. *When you rose from the dead, Jesus, you went first to see your Mother. May*

she hold first place in my Heart after you.

2. THE ASCENSION into Heaven took place forty days after Easter. Christ is now in glory enthroned at the right hand of His Eternal Father. *By contemplating Heaven, may we learn the little worth of the things of the world.*

3. THE DESCENT OF THE HOLY SPIRIT took place at Pentecost, fifty days after Easter, when He came upon the Apostles in the form of fiery tongues. *Ask for an increase of divine love.*

4. THE ASSUMPTION - At the close of her life on earth, Mary was taken body and soul into Heaven, there to intercede for us. *Ask for the grace of final perseverance.*

5. THE CORONATION - Mary is Queen of the Universe and our loving Mother. *Ask her to make you a saint.*

THE HAIL HOLY QUEEN

(Prayer recited after the Rosary)

Hail Holy Queen, Mother of mercy, our life, our sweetness and our hope! To Thee do we cry, poor banished children of Eve; to Thee do we send up our sighs, our mourning, and weeping in this valley of tears! Turn, then, most gracious Advocate, Thine eyes of mercy toward us; and after this, and during our exile, show unto us the blessed fruit of Thy womb, Jesus. O clement, O loving, O sweet Virgin Mary...

Priest: Pray for us, O Queen of the Most Holy Rosary.

People: That we may be made worthy of the promises of Christ.

Priest: Let us pray...

O God, Whose only-begotten Son, by His life, death and resurrection, has purchased for us the rewards of eternal life, grant, we beseech Thee, that meditating upon these mysteries of the most holy rosary of the Blessed Virgin Mary, we may imitate what they contain, and obtain what they promise. Through the same Christ, our Lord. Amen.

BAPTISM OF THE UNBORN

For the spiritual adoption of an unborn child, sprinkle Holy Water in all directions and then say:

"I baptise you, (child's name - preferably one of a saint) in the name of the Father, and of the Son and of the Holy Spirit. Amen. In the name of Jesus (and Mary), I release you to God, our Father. Through the Holy Spirit, I pray also for the release of all grief and guilt in your parents and those associated with this abortion. Go now in peace to the place prepared for you in our Father's house. Amen."

TANTUM ERGO

Tantum Ergo Sacramentum
Veneremus cernui:
Et antiquum documentum
Novo cedat ritui:
Praestat fides supplementum
Sensuum defectui
Genitori, Genitoque
Laus et jubilatio
Salus, honor, virtus quoque
Sit et benedictio
Procedenti ab utroque
Compar sit laudatio. Amen.

Priest: Panem de coelo praestitisti eis.
People: Omne delectamentum in se habentem.

Priest: Oremus: Deus, qui nobis sub Sacramento mirabili passionis tuae memoriam reliquisti; tribue, quaesumus, ita nos Corporis et Sanguinis tui sacra mysteria venerari, ut redemptionis tuae fructum in nobis jugiter sentiamus. Qui vivis et regnas in saecula saeculorum.
People: Amen.

THE DIVINE PRAISES

Blessed be God.
Blessed be His Holy Name.
Blessed be Jesus Christ, true God and true Man.

Blessed be the Name of Jesus.

Blessed be His Most Holy Face.

Blessed be His Most Sacred Heart.

Blessed be His Most Precious Blood.

Blessed be Jesus in the Most Holy Sacrament of the Altar.

Blessed be the Holy Spirit, the Consoler.

Blessed be the great Mother of God, Mary most holy.

Blessed be her holy and Immaculate Conception.

Blessed be her Glorious Assumption

Blessed be the name of Mary, Virgin and Mother.

Blessed be good St. Joseph, her most chaste Spouse.

Blessed be God in His Angels and in His Saints.

ACT OF CONSECRATION

O Lord Jesus, we believe most firmly in You, we love You. You are the Eternal Son of God and the Son Incarnate of the Blessed Virgin Mary. You are the Lord and Absolute Ruler of all creation. We acknowledge You, therefore, as the Universal Sovereign of all creatures. You are the Lord and Supreme Ruler of all mankind, and we, in acknowledging this Your dominion, consecrate ourselves to You now and forever. Loving Jesus, we place our families under the protection of Your Holy Face, and of Your Virgin Mother, Mary most sorrowful. We promise to be faithful to You for the rest of our lives and to observe with fidelity Your Holy Commandments. We will never deny before others, You and Your Divine rights over us and all humankind. Grant us the grace to never sin again; nevertheless, should we fail, O Divine Saviour, have mercy on us and restore us to Your grace. Radiate Your Divine Countenance upon us and bless us now and forever. Embrace us at the hour of death in Your Kingdom for all eternity, through the intercession of Your Blessed Mother, of all Your Saints who behold You in Heaven, and the just who glorify You on earth. O Jesus, be mindful of us forever and never forsake us; protect our families. O Mother of Sorrows, by the eternal glory which you enjoy in Heaven, through the merits of your bitter anguish in the Sacred Passion of your Beloved Son, our Lord Jesus Christ, obtain for us the grace that the Precious Blood shed by Jesus for the redemption of our souls, be not shed for us in vain. We love you, O Mary. Embrace us and bless us, O Mother. Protect us in life and in death. Amen.

Glory be to the Father, and to the Son, and to the Holy Spirit. As it was in the beginning, is now, and will be forever. Amen.

Section III :
Mass, Occasional Prayers & Hymns

MASS IN HONOR of THE MOST HOLY FACE of OUR LORD JESUS CHRIST

(Permission granted by the Holy See
April 17, 1958)

OPENING PRAYER

Lord Jesus Christ, whose Holy Face hidden in Your Passion, shines like the sun in its splendor, deign to grant us, who unite ourselves on earth to Your sufferings, to rejoice in Heaven in the revelation of Your glory. You who live and reign with the Father and the Holy Spirit, one God, for ever and ever. Amen.

FIRST READING (Num. 21)

When those that were afflicted looked upon it, they were healed.

A reading from the book of Numbers:

The people lost patience. They spoke against God and against Moses, "Why did you bring us out of Egypt to die in this wilderness? For there is neither bread nor water here; we are sick of this unsatisfying food."

At this, God sent fiery serpents among the people; their bite brought death to many in Israel. The people came and said to Moses, "We have sinned by speaking against the Lord and against you. Intercede for us with the Lord to save us from these serpents."

Moses interceded for the people, and the Lord answered him, "Make a fiery serpent and put it on a standard. If anyone is bitten and looks at it, he shall live."

So Moses fashioned a bronze serpent which he put on a standard, and if anyone was bitten by a serpent, he looked at the bronze serpent and lived. *The word of the Lord.*

RESPONSORIAL PSALM - Ps. 77 (78)

Response: Never forget the deeds of the Lord.

Give heed, my people, to my teaching;
turn your ear to the words of my mouth.
I will open my mouth in a parable
and reveal hidden lessons of the past.   RESP.

When he slew them, then they would seek him,
return and seek him in earnest.
They would remember that God was their rock,
God, the Most High their redeemer.   RESP.

But the words they spoke were mere flattery;
they lied to him with their lips.
For their hearts were not truly with him;
they were not faithful to his covenant.   RESP.

Yet he who is full of compassion

forgave their sin and spared them.

So often he held back his anger

when he might have stirred up his rage.　　RESP.

SECOND READING (Phil. 2)

He humbled himself, therefore God has exalted him.

A reading from the letter of Paul to the Philippians:

The state of Christ Jesus was divine,

yet he did not cling to his equality with God

but emptied himself to assume the condition of a slave, and became as men are;

and being as all men are, he was humbler yet,

even to accepting death, death on a cross.

But God raised him high and gave him the name

which is above all other names

so that all beings

in the heavens, on earth and in the underworld,

should bend the knee at the name of Jesus

and that every tongue should acclaim

Jesus Christ as Lord,

to the glory of God, the Father. *The word of the Lord.*

GOSPEL ACCLAMATION

We adore you, O Christ, and we praise you, because by your cross you have redeemed the world.

THE GOSPEL (John 3)

The Son of Man must be lifted up.

A reading from the holy gospel according to John:

Jesus said to Nicodemus:

"No one has gone up to heaven

except the one who came down from heaven,

the Son of Man who is in heaven;

and the Son of Man must be lifted up

as Moses lifted up the serpent in the desert,

so that everyone who believes may have eternal life in him.

Yes, God loved the world so much that he gave his only Son,

so that everyone who believes in him may not be lost but may have eternal life.

For God sent his Son into the world

not to condemn the world,

but so that through him, the world might be saved."

Praise to you, Lord Jesus Christ.

PRAYER OVER THE GIFTS

O God, our protector, regard and consider the Face of your Christ, who offers Himself to You as Immaculate Victim, in our favour, and grant us that offering You the same Immaculate Victim, we also may become a holocaust pleasing to You. And we ask you this in the Name of Jesus Christ, Your Son, Our Lord, who lives and reigns for ever and ever. Amen.

PRAYER AFTER COMMUNION

We beg You, Lord, in your mercy, to cause the light of your Face to shine upon us, so that, instructed by your justice, we may be able to despise the world's seductions and triumph over its actions. You who live and reign for ever and ever. Amen.

For Holy Hour of Reparation, please return to page 31)

BLESSING OF THE HOLY FACE

May the Lord bless you and keep you;

May the Lord let His Face shine on you and be gracious to you;

May the Lord uncover His Face to you and bring you peace.

LITANY OF OUR LADY

Lord, have mercy on us.

Christ, have mercy on us.

Lord have mercy on us. Christ, hear us.

Christ, graciously hear us.

God, the Father of Heaven, *have mercy on us.*

God, the Son, Redeemer of the world,

have mercy on us.

God, the Holy Spirit, *have mercy on us.*

Holy Trinity, One God, *have mercy on us.*

Holy Mary, *pray for us.*

Holy Mother of God, *pray for us.*

Holy Virgin of virgins, *pray for us.*

Mother of Christ, *pray for us.*

Mother of divine grace,	*pray for us.*
Mother most pure,	*pray for us.*
Mother most chaste,	*pray for us.*
Mother inviolate,	*pray for us.*
Mother undefiled,	*pray for us.*
Mother most amiable,	*pray for us.*
Mother most admirable,	*pray for us.*
Mother of good counsel,	*pray for us.*
Mother of our Creator,	*pray for us.*
Mother of our Saviour,	*pray for us.*
Virgin most prudent,	*pray for us.*
Virgin most venerable,	*pray for us.*
Virgin most renowned,	*pray for us.*
Virgin most powerful,	*pray for us.*
Virgin most merciful,	*pray for us.*
Virgin most faithful,	*pray for us.*
Mirror of justice,	*pray for us.*
Seat of wisdom,	*pray for us.*
Cause of our joy,	*pray for us.*
Spiritual vessel,	*pray for us.*
Vessel of honor,	*pray for us.*
Singular vessel of devotion,	*pray for us.*
Mystical rose,	*pray for us.*
Tower of David,	*pray for us.*
Tower of ivory,	*pray for us.*
House of gold,	*pray for us.*
Ark of the covenant,	*pray for us.*
Gate of Heaven,	*pray for us.*

Morning star,	*pray for us.*
Health of the sick,	*pray for us.*
Refuge of sinners,	*pray for us.*
Comforter of the afflicted,	*pray for us.*
Help of Christians,	*pray for us.*
Queen of angels,	*pray for us.*
Queen of patriarchs,	*pray for us.*
Queen of prophets,	*pray for us.*
Queen of apostles,	*pray for us.*
Queen of martyrs,	*pray for us.*
Queen of confessors,	*pray for us.*
Queen of virgins,	*pray for us.*
Queen of all saints,	*pray for us.*
Queen conceived without original sin,	*pray for us.*
Queen assumed into Heaven,	*pray for us.*
Queen of the most holy Rosary,	*pray for us.*
Queen of peace,	*pray for us.*

Lamb of God, Who take away
   the sins of the world, *spare us, O Lord.*

Lamb of God, Who take away the
   sins of the world, *graciously hear us, O Lord.*

Lamb of God, Who take away
   the sins of the world, *have mercy on us.*

Priest: Pray for us, O holy Mother of God.

All: That we may be made worthy of the promises of Christ.

Priest: Let us pray. Pour forth, we beseech you, O Lord, your grace into our hearts; that as we have known the incarnation of Christ your Son by the message of an angel, so, by His Passion and Cross, we may be brought to the glory of the Resurrection; through the same Christ, our Lord.

All: Amen.

PRAYER TO THE INFANT JESUS OF PRAGUE

O merciful Infant Jesus! I know of Thy miraculous deeds for the sick...in view of the innumerable graces and the cures granted...through the veneration of Thy Holy Infancy, particularily in the statue of Prague...I exclaim with the greatest assurance: O most loving Infant Jesus, Thou canst cure me if Thou wilt! Extend Thy holy hand and by Thy power take away all pain and infirmity. Amen.

Our Lord to St. Theresa of Avila:

"The more you honor Me, the more I will bless you! Occupy yourself with My interests and I will occupy Myself with yours."

PRAYER TO ST. THERESE, THE LITTLE FLOWER

O Little Therese of the Child Jesus, please pick for me a rose from the heavenly gardens and send it to me as a message of love. O Little Flower of Jesus, ask God today to grant the favors I now place with confidence in your hands...(mention specific request). St. Therese, help me to always believe as you did, in God's great love for me, so that I might imitate your "Little Way" each day. Amen.

OUR LADY OF GUADALUPE
INTERCESSOR OF THE UNBORN
Please see page 56 to adopt an unborn child.

PRAYER TO OUR LADY OF GUADALUPE

(Patroness of the Unborn)

To help stop the anti-life push in the U.S., Archbishop Fulton J. Sheen encouraged the spiritual adoption of an unborn child. This is done by praying that one particular but unknown child's life be spared abortion and be allowed to continue to and after birth. To help accomplish this, it was recommended that an individual say the following daily prayer for a period of one year:

"Jesus, Mary and Jospeh, I love you very much. I beg you to spare the life of the unborn baby that I have spiritually adopted who is in danger of abortion."

During your earthly life, this spiritually adopted child of yours will be known only to God, but in the world to come and throughout eternity, both you and the child will find happiness in each other's company.

THE POWERFUL SACRAMENT OF CONFESSION

The powerful Sacrament of Confession is the means instituted by our Divine Saviour to help us attain once again the state of Sanctifying Grace when we have lost it by committing mortal sin. It is also an effective means to help us overcome our venial sins.

ACT OF CONTRITION

O my God, I am heartily sorry for having offended Thee, and I detest all my sins, because I dread the loss of Heaven and the pains of Hell, but most of all because they offend Thee, my God, who are all-good and deserving of all my love. I firmly

56

resolve, with the help of your grace, to confess my sins, to do penance and to amend my life. Amen.

PRAYER TO ST. DISMAS, THE GOOD THIEF

Glorious St. Dismas, you alone of all the great Penitent Saints were directly canonized by Christ Himself; you were assured of a place in Heaven with Him "this day" because of the sincere confession of your sins to Him in the tribunal of Calvary and your true sorrow for them as you hung beside Him in that open confessional; you who by the direct sword thrust of your love and repentance did open the Heart of Jesus in mercy and forgiveness even before the centurion's spear tore it asunder; you whose face was closer to that of Jesus in His last agony, to offer Him a word of comfort, closer even than that of His Beloved Mother, Mary; you who knew so well how to pray, teach me the words to say to Him to gain pardon and the grace of perseverance; and you who are so close to Him now in Heaven, as you were during His last moments on earth, pray to Him for me that I shall never again desert Him, but that at the close of my life, I may hear from Him the words He addressed to you: "This day, thou shalt be with Me in Paradise." (Feast Day is on April 24th.) Amen.

PRAYER TO ST. MICHAEL

St. Michael, the Archangel, defend us in the day of battle; be our safeguard against the wickedness and snares of the devil. May God rebuke him, we humbly pray, and do Thou, O prince of the Heavenly Host, by the power of God, cast into Hell, Satan and all the other evil spirits, who prowl throughout the world, seeking the ruin of souls. Amen.

PRAYER TO OUR GUARDIAN ANGEL

Angel of God, my guardian dear, to whom God's love commits me here, ever this day be at my side, to light and guard, to rule and guide. Amen.

PRAYER OF THE HOLY MAN OF TOURS

Oh Saviour Jesus! At the sight of Thy most Holy Face disfigured by suffering, at the sight of Thy Sacred Heart so full of love, I exclaim with Saint Augustine, "Lord Jesus, imprint upon my heart Thy sacred wounds, that I may read therein both Thy sorrow and thy love - thy sorrow, that for Thy sake I may suffer all grief, and Thy love, that for Thy sake I may despise all other love." Lord Jesus, in presenting myself before Thy adorable Face to beg of Thee the graces we are in need of, we entreat of Thee, above all things, to give us an interior disposition never to refuse Thee anything which Thou mayst daily ask of us, by means of Thy holy commandments and Thy divine inspirations. Amen.

THE CHAPLET (OR CROWN)
OF THE HOLY FACE

The fourteen beads which form the Chaplet of the Holy Face are to remind us of the fourteen stations of the WAY to THE CROSS. This is how it is prayed:

Recite the following prayer while:

1- keeping one's eyes on the picture of the Holy Face of Jesus.

2- venerating the Medal of the Holy Face of Jesus

(it shows the Holy Face on one side and a Sacred Host on the other).

3- holding one's arms stretched as in the shape of a Cross (the sick and the handicapped are exempt):

Eternal Father,

For my own salvation and the salvation of all men, I offer you the infinite merits of your beloved SON, JESUS CHRIST, whose HOLY FACE unveils to us your FATHERLY MERCY as well as your GODLY presence. It is He who told us, "WHO SEES ME, SEES THE FATHER."

Through the SORROWFUL, IMMACULATE and MERCIFUL HEART of MARY, your beloved DAUGHTER, the faithful and ever VIRGIN SPOUSE of the HOLY SPIRIT and MOTHER of your SON, our LORD and REDEEMER, I offer you the infinite merits which the HOLY FACE of JESUS has earned for us.

I offer them also through ST. JOSEPH, the faithful manager of all the gifts and favours coming from you, the FATHER of LIGHT and MERCY. I also express my THANKFULNESS for the HOLY FACE of JESUS, our mediator, who protects us against every interior and exterior harm.

4- then, on each and every one of the fourteen beads, recite the following invocation:

"LET THE LIGHT OF YOUR HOLY FACE SHINE ON US, AND IN YOUR MERCY SAVE US."

PRAYER TO ST. JUDE

(To be said in cases despaired of)

St. Jude, glorious Apostle, faithful servant and friend of Jesus, the name of the traitor has caused you to be forgotten by many, but the true Church invokes you universally as the Patron of things despaired of; pray for me, who am so miserable; pray for me, that finally I may receive the consolations and the succor of Heaven in all my necessities, tribulations and sufferings particularily (here make your request), and that I may bless God with the Elect throughout Eternity. Amen.

St. Jude, Apostle, martyr and relative of our Lord Jesus Christ, of Mary and of Joseph, intercede for us.

PRAYER TO OUR MOTHER OF PERPETUAL HELP

O Mother of perpetual help, many are your devout children who surround your holy picture, imploring your assistance. We bless you as our assured help. We already feel the benefit of your maternal protection. With confidence we present ourselves before you in our many needs. You know the many evils to which we are exposed; our many spiritual and temporal needs. Trials and sorrows are often our lot; misfortunes and privations are ever before us; the cross is our daily companion. Look upon us with eyes of pity, most compassionate mother, and keep us ever in your care. At this moment, I ask especially for this necessity (make your intention). Help me, O my mother, in all needs. Deliver me from all my ills. In all things, help me to conform to the will of Thy Divine Son. With faith, hope and love, I seek a

Divine answer to my prayer through you, O Mother of Perpetual Help. Amen.

A PRAYER FOR THE POPE

Almighty and everlasting God, have mercy upon your servant N., our Supreme Pontiff, and direct him, according to your loving kindness, in the way of eternal salvation; that, of your gift, he may ever desire that which is pleasing to You and may accomplish it with all his might. Through Christ, our Lord. Amen. (Roman Ritual)

Lord Jesus, shelter our Holy Father, the Pope, under the protection of your Sacred Heart. Be his light, his strength and his consolation. (Raccolta)

A PRAYER FOR THE CLERGY

Almighty and eternal God, look upon the Face of your Son and for love of Him, have pity on your priests. Remember that they are weak and frail human beings like ourselves. Keep them close to You so that they may never do anything unworthy of their sublime vocation. Help them to lead us in the footsteps of your Son, Jesus Christ, our Lord. Amen.

THE FOUR KEYS TO HEAVEN:

Mass

Rosary

Scapular

Way Of The Cross

How to Pray the Rosary:

1. Make the Sign of the Cross and pray the "Apostle's Creed."
2. Pray the "Our Father."
3. Pray three "Hail Mary's."
4. Pray the "Glory be to the Father."
5. Announce the First Mystery; then pray the "Our Father."
6. Pray ten "Hail Mary's" while meditating on the Mystery.
7. Pray the "Glory Be to the Father."
8. Announce the Second Mystery; then pray the "Our Father". Repeat steps 6 and 7 and continue with the Third, Fourth, and Fifth Mysteries in the same manner.
9. In conclusion, recite the "Hail Holy Queen."

Prayers For The Rosary

THE SIGN OF THE CROSS

In the name of the Father, and of the Son, and of the Holy Spirit. Amen.

THE APOSTLE'S CREED

believe in God, the Father Almighty, Creator of Heaven and earth; and in Jesus Christ, His only Son, our Lord; who was conceived by the power of the Holy Spirit, born of the Virgin Mary, suffered under Pontius Pilate, was crucified, died and was buried. He decended into hell; on the third day, He rose again from the dead; He ascended into Heaven, and sits at the right hand of God, the Father Almighty; from thence, He shall come to judge the living and the dead.

believe in the Holy Spirit, the Holy Catholic Church, the communion of saints, the forgiveness of sins, the resurrection of the body and life everlasting. Amen.

THE OUR FATHER

Our Father, who art in Heaven, hallowed be Thy name; Thy kingdom come; Thy will be done on earth as it is in Heaven.

Give us this day our daily bread; and forgive us our trespasses, as we forgive those who trespass against us; and lead us not into temptation, but deliver us from evil. Amen.

THE HAIL MARY

Hail Mary, full of grace, the Lord is with thee! Blessed art thou among women, and blessed is the fruit of thy womb, Jesus. Holy Mary, Mother of God, pray for us sinners, now, and at the hour of our death. Amen.

GLORY BE TO THE FATHER

Glory be to the Father, and to the Son, and to the Holy Spirit, as it was in the beginning, is now, and ever shall be, world without end. Amen.

THE FATIMA ASPIRATION

(At the close of each decade)

O my Jesus, forgive us our sins, save us from the fire of hell and lead all souls to Heaven, especially those who have most need of Thy mercy.

THE HAIL HOLY QUEEN

(Prayer after the Rosary)

Hail Holy Queen, Mother of mercy, our life, our sweetness and our hope! To Thee do we cry, poor banished children of Eve; to Thee do we send up our sighs, our mourning, and weeping in this valley of tears! Turn, then, most gracious Advocate, Thine eyes of mercy toward us; and after this, and during our exile, show unto us the blessed fruit of Thy womb, Jesus. O clement, O loving, O sweet Virgin Mary. Pray for us, O Queen of the most Holy Rosary. That we may be made worthy of the promises of Christ. Amen.

THE MEMORARE

Remember, O most gracious Virgin Mary, that never was it known that anyone who fled to your protection, implored your help, or sought your intercession, was left unaided. Inspired with this confidence, I fly unto you, O Virgin of virgins and Mother; to you I come, before you I stand, sinful and sorrowful. O Mother of the Word Incarnate, despise not my petitions, but in your mercy, hear and answer me. Amen.

YOUR KEY TO HEAVEN

The Rosary is a key to Heaven. It is not a charm or talisman, but a way of life, and a means of eternal salvation. It is a way of life because it teaches you - kneeling, childlike before Our Blessed Mother - Christ who is the Life of the World and to know whom is eternal life. The Rosary is a means of salvation because a true child of Mary is never lost, and one who says the Rosary daily is truly Mary's child. Recite it, then, daily and devoutly, simply because Our Blessed Mother asked it of us all when she came to Fatima.

Obedience to our Heavenly Mother and Blessed Rosary Queen is reason enough for reciting it.

In the Holy Rosary, you will find a solution for all your problems, no matter how big and difficult and humanly impossible they may be - for Mary is our all-powerful Advocate and she can obtain from the Heart of her Divine Son whatever is good for her children.

And so the Rosary proves to be a path of true peace and the way to Heaven. Say it first of all for yourself and then, when through it you have been fully "converted" and turned fully to God, say it for the conversion of all poor sinners the world over. No one is beyond redemption if he but turns to Mary Immaculate. Taking her Rosary, keeping it with you and reciting it each day, is, in truth, turning to Mary. She will crush the serpent's head. Our Lady of the Most Holy Rosary is Our Lady of Victory, for through the Rosary she is victorious in all the battles of God - your own included.

WHO can pray the Rosary:

Anyone, be he man, woman, or child, Jew or Gentile, teenager or adult, athlete or invalid, professor or politician, saint or sinner, celebrity, scientist or receptionist, barmaid, alchoholic or drug addict - all are children of Mary Immaculate and all are in need of her help to get to Heaven.

WHERE to pray the Rosary:

In the church before Jesus hidden in the Blessed Sacrament, before Our Lady's shrine whether in the church or at home, behind the wheel of your car in a cross-country drive or as you walk down a city street - anywhere and everywhere the Rosary may be said.

WHEN to pray the Rosary:

At morning, noon and night (especially if you say five decades at each of these three periods, completing the fifteen in a day); in time of sorrow, danger or temptation; on occasions of joy, thanksgiving or jubilee; with the Rosary broadcast or in the sacred family circle; in a cell of solitary confinement; at night when you cannot sleep; while waiting for a bus or in a doctor's office... Turn off the TV or radio, lift up your hearts, and with the holy angels, tune in on the court of Heaven as you softly repeat: "Hail Mary ... Holy Mary ... pray for us now, and at the hour of our death."

HOW to pray the Rosary:

The prayers are written out for you here in this booklet. Saying them daily, you will soon know them by heart, even though they may be new to you now. The scenes of Our Lord's life and of Our Lady's are suggested here. Ponder successively each scene as if you were really present while it was taking place and apply it to yourself as you say the Our Father, the ten Hail Mary's, the Glory Be, and the post-decade petition taught us by Our Lady at Fatima, on each of the five decades of the three sets of scenes (or mysteries): the joyful, the sorrowful, and the glorious mysteries.

If you say five decades a day, recite the Joyful Mysteries on Mondays and Thursdays; the Sorrowful on Tuesdays and Fridays; the Glorious on Wednesdays, Saturdays and Sundays. This is all you need just now. Go on from here and ask St. Joseph and your Guardian Angel to make you a great lover of the Holy Rosary and through it, a true child of Mary. With the Rosary, you will tread life's paths in peace for you are following Christ who is the Way, the Truth and the Life while you clasp in your hand a veritable Key to Heaven. The Blessed Virgin Mary said to Saint Dominic, *"One day, through the Rosary and the Scapular, I will save the world."*

THE BROWN SCAPULAR OF OUR LADY
OF MOUNT CARMEL

(A gift to you from your Heavenly Mother)

"Whosoever dies clothed in this (scapular) shall not suffer eternal fire." This is the Blessed Virgin Mary's promise, made July 16, 1251, to St. Simon Stock.

It is an assurance of salvation.

Love the Scapular.

Wear it always.

Venerate it often.

True devotion to Mary consists in three things: VENERATION, CONFIDENCE and LOVE. Without saying to Mary that we venerate her, love her, and trust in her protection, we tell her these things every moment of the day by simply wearing the Scapular.

The Sabbatine Privilege is Mary's promise to release from Purgatory soon after death all those who:

1. Wear the Brown Scapular.

2. Observe chastity according to their state in life.

3. Say the Little Office of the Blessed Virgin Mary every day (or Rosary).

The Fifteen Promises of Mary to Christians Who Recite the Rosary

1. Whoever shall faithfully serve me by the recitation of the rosary shall receive signal graces.

2. I promise my special protection and the greatest graces to all those who shall recite the rosary.

3. The rosary shall be a powerful armour against hell, it will destroy vice, decrease sin, and defeat heresies.

4. It will cause virtue and good works to flourish; it will obtain for souls the abundant mercy of God; it will withdraw the hearts of men from the love of the world and its vanities, and will lift them to the desire of eternal things. Oh, that souls would sanctify themselves by this means.

5. The soul which recommends itself to me by reciting the rosary shall not perish.

6. Whoever shall recite the rosary devoutly, applying himself to the consideration of its sacred mysteries shall never be conquered by misfortune. God will not chastise him in His justice, he shall not perish by an unprovided death; if he be just, he shall remain in the grace of God, and become worthy of eternal life.

7. Whoever shall have a true devotion for the rosary shall not die without the sacraments of the Church.

8. Those who are faithful to the rosary shall have during their life and death the light of God and the plentitude of His graces; at death, they shall participate in the merits of the saints in Paradise.

9. I shall deliver from Purgatory those who have been devoted to the rosary.

10. The faithful children of the rosary shall merit a high degree of glory in Heaven.

11. You shall obtain all you ask of me by the recitation of the rosary.

12. All those who propogate the holy rosary shall be aided by me in their necessities.

13. I have obtained from my Divine Son that all the advocates of the rosary shall have for intercessors the entire celestial court during their life and at the hour of death.

14. All who recite the rosary are my sons and daughters; brothers and sisters of my only son Jesus Christ.

15. Devotion of my rosary is a great sign of predestination.

UNFAILING PRAYER TO ST. ANTHONY

"Blessed be God in His Angels and in His Saints"

O Holy St. Anthony, gentlest of Saints, your love for God and Charity for His creatures made you worthy, when on earth, to possess miraculous powers. Miracles waited on your word, which you were ever ready to speak for those in trouble or anxiety. Encouraged by this thought, I implore of you to obtain for me (request). The answer to my prayer may require a miracle, even so, you are the Saint of Miracles. O gentle and loving St. Anthony, whose heart was ever full of human sympathy, whisper my petition into the ears of the Sweet Infant Jesus, who loved to be folded in your arms; and the gratitude of my heart will ever be yours. (13 Paters, Aves and Glorias)

PRAYER OF ST. GERTRUDE

O Lord Jesus, delightful and majestic is Your Countenance, where there radiates the beauteous aura of the divinity. Incline Your adorable Face towards me that I may draw so close as not to be near but rather within You. When will I come to contemplate that coveted, desirable and adorable Face of my Jesus, whose beauty my soul has long thirsted to behold? When will I appear before Your throne to look upon Your delightful Face, whose divine splendour in itself fulfills the desire of the saints and brings forth praises of exaltation from the heart and lips? Grant forthwith, that I may be hastily delivered from this land of exile, that I may behold Your most gentle Countenance. How can eyes be satiated in beholding and ears in hearing of the glory of Your Countenance! Without You, Heaven and earth and all things are like total bleakness. Your adorable Face alone is my solace and the placidness of Spring. O Jesus, sprinkle my members with the blood that streams from the wounds of Your glorious Head, crowned with thorns. The ineffable perfume of that blood and of those sufferings shall banish slothfulness and torpidity from the soul and adorn it anew, as it comes to pass in the Springtime when the frost of Winter is over. Amen.

The Twelve Promises of the Sacred Heart to St. Margaret Mary

1. I will grant them all the graces necessary for their state of life.

2. I will give peace in their families.

3. I will console them in all their troubles.

4. They shall find in My Heart an assured refuge during life and especially at the hour of death.

5. I will pour abundant blessings on all their undertakings.

6. Sinners shall find in My Heart the source and infinite ocean of mercy.

7. Tepid souls shall become fervent.

8. Fervent souls shall speedily rise to great perfection.

9. I will bless the homes in which the image of My Sacred Heart shall be exposed and honoured.

10. I will give to priests the power to touch the most hardened hearts.

11. Those who propogate this devotion shall have their name written in My Heart, and it shall never be effaced.

12. The all-powerful love of My Heart will grant to all those who shall receive Communion on the First Friday of nine consecutive months the grace of final repentance; they shall not die under My displeasure, nor without receiving their Sacraments; My Heart shall be their assured refuge at that last hour.

"And He showed me that it was His great desire of being loved by all and of withdrawing them from the path of ruin into which Satan hurls crowds of them, that made Him form the design of manifesting His Heart to us, with all the treasures of love, of mercy, of grace, of sanctification and salvation which it contains, in order that those who desire to render Him and procure for Him all the honour and love possible, might themselves be abundantly enriched with those divine treasures of which this Heart is the source. He should be honoured under the figure of this Heart of flesh, and its image should be exposed...He promised me that wherever this image should be exposed with a view to showing it special honour, He would pour forth His blessings and graces. This devotion was the last effort of His love that He would grant to all in these latter ages, in order to withdraw them from the empire of Satan which He desired to destroy, and thus to introduce them into the sweet liberty of the rule of His love, which He wished to restore in the hearts of all those who should embrace this devotion."

(St. Margaret Mary)

PRAYER TO RECEIVE HELP FROM THE
SACRED HEART OF JESUS

Take away, O my Jesus, the blindness of my heart, that I may know Thee; take away the hardness of my heart, that I may fear Thee; take away the coldness of my heart, that I may love Thee; take away the weakness of my heart, that I may resist everything that is contrary to Thy will; take away its heavy, earthly sluggishness and selfishness, that I may be capable of heroic sacrifice for Thy glory, and for the souls whom Thou hast redeemed with Thy own most Precious Blood. Amen.

UNFAILING PRAYER TO THE BLESSED VIRGIN MARY

(Never found to fail)

O Most beautiful Flower of Mount Carmel, Fruitful Vine, Splendour of Heaven, Blessed Mother of the Son of God, Immaculate Virgin, assist me in this my necessity. O Star of the Sea, help me and show me herein you are my Mother. O Holy Mary, Mother of God, Queen of Heaven and Earth, I humbly beseech you from the bottom of my heart, to succour me in this necessity; there are none that can withstand your power.

O, show me herein you are my Mother. O Mary, conceived without sin, pray for us who have recourse to thee. Sweet Mother, I place this cause in your hands.

(3 times).

Our Lord to Sister Mary of St. Peter:

"Apply yourself to honour My Heart and that of My Mother. Do not separate them."

The Ten Commandments of God

I. I am the Lord thy God; thou shalt not have strange gods before Me.

II. Thou shalt not take the name of the Lord thy God in vain.

III. Remember thou keep holy the Lord's day.

IV. Honor thy father and thy mother.

V. Thou shalt not kill.

VI. Thou shalt not commit adultery.

VII. Thou shalt not steal.

VIII. Thou shalt not bear false witness against thy neighbor.

IX. Thou shalt not covet thy neighbor's wife.

X. Thou shalt not covet thy neighbor's goods.

The Six Chief Precepts of the Church

1. To assist at Mass on all Sundays and Holy Days of obligation.

2. To fast and to abstain on the days appointed.

3. To confess our sins at least once a year.

4. To receive Holy Communion during Easter time.

5. To contribute to the support of the Church.

6. To observe the laws of the Church concerning marriage.

THE BLOOD OF CHRIST

Life had to be forfeited for our sins, and no life is more precious than that of God who became man. His blood was the blood of the God-man, and therefore he paid the infinite price. We were not bought with gold and silver, but with the precious blood of Christ. That is how our sins are forgiven, and that is why our blessed Lord prayed for our forgiveness at the moment that he poured out his blood for us sinners. If you have faith in Jesus' sacrifice, now is the time to go to confession, to get rid of your sins. When the priest raises his hands in absolution over you, the blood of Christ is dripping from his fingers. We priests are hardly conscious of this great power. I think we would almost be shocked to death if we ever really realized it. But that is how the sin is absolved, by this blood of Christ. (The late Archbishop Fulton J. Sheen).

A SHORT WAY OF THE CROSS

(As used by the Franciscan Fathers on their Missions)

FIRST STATION: Jesus Condemned to Death

Oh Jesus, so meek and uncomplaining, teach me resignation in trials.

SECOND STATION: Jesus Carries His Cross

My Jesus, this Cross should be mine, not Thine; my sins crucified Thee.

THIRD STATION: Our Lord Falls the First Time

O Jesus! By this first fall, never let me fall into mortal sin.

FOURTH STATION: Jesus Meets His Mother

O Jesus! May no human tie, however dear, keep me from following the road of the Cross.

FIFTH STATION: Simon the Cyrenean Helps Jesus Carry His Cross

Simon unwillingly assisted Thee; may I, with patience, suffer all for Thee.

SIXTH STATION: Veronica Wipes the Face of Jesus

O Jesus! Thou didst imprint Thy sacred features upon Veronica's veil; stamp them also indelibly upon my heart.

SEVENTH STATION: The Second Fall of Jesus

By Thy second fall, preserve me, dear Lord, from relapse into sin.

EIGHTH STATION: Jesus Consoles the Women of Jerusalem

My greatest consolation would be to hear Thee say: "Many sins are forgiven thee, because thou hast loved much."

NINTH STATION: The Third Fall of Jesus

O Jesus! When weary upon life's long journey, be Thou my strength and my perseverance.

TENTH STATION: Jesus Stripped of His Garments

My soul has been robbed of its robe of innocence; clothe me, dear Jesus, with the garb of penance and contrition.

ELEVENTH STATION: Jesus Nailed to the Cross

Thou didst forgive Thy enemies; my God, teach me to forgive injuries and FORGET them.

TWELFTH STATION: Jesus Dies on the Cross

Thou art dying, my Jesus, but Thy Sacred Heart still throbs with love for Thy sinful children.

THIRTEENTH STATION: Jesus Taken Down from the Cross

Receive me into thy arms, O Sorrowful Mother; and obtain for me perfect contrition for my sins.

FOURTEENTH STATION: Jesus Laid in the Sepulchre

When I receive Thee into my heart in Holy Communion, O Jesus, make it a fit abiding place for Thy adorable Body. Amen.

COME HOLY GHOST

Come, Holy Ghost, Creator blest,
And in our hearts take up Thy rest;
Come with Thy grace and heav'nly aid
To fill the hearts which Thou hast made,
To fill the hearts which Thou hast made.

O Comforter, to Thee we cry,
Thou gift of God sent from on high,
Thou font of life and fire of love,
The soul's anointing from above,
The soul's anointing from above.

Praise be to Thee, Father and Son,
And Holy Spirit, with them one;
And may the Son on us bestow
All gifts that from the Spirit flow,
All gifts that from the Spirit flow.

PRAYER OF ST. FRANCIS

Lord, make me a channel of Your peace.
Where there is hatred, let me bring Your love.
Where there is injury, your pardon, Lord.
And where there is doubt, true faith in You.

Lord, make me a channel of Your peace.
Where there is despair in life, let me bring hope.
Where there is darkness, only light,
And where there is sadness, ever joy.

Oh, Master, grant that I may never seek
So much to be consoled, as to console.
To be understood, as to understand.
To be loved, as to love with all my soul.

Lord, make me a channel of Your peace.
It is in pardoning that we are pardoned.
In giving to all men, that we receive
And in dying that we are born into eternal life

IMMACULATE MARY

Immaculate Mary, your praises we sing.
You reign now in splendour with Jesus, our King.
Ave, Ave, Ave Maria!
Ave, Ave Maria!

In Heaven the blessed, your glory proclaim.
On earth, we, your children, invoke your sweet name.
Ave, Ave, Ave Maria!
Ave, Ave Maria!

We pray for the Church,
Our true mother on earth,
And beg you to watch o'er the land of our birth.
Ave, Ave, Ave Maria!
Ave, Ave Maria!

HOLY GOD, WE PRAISE THY NAME

Holy God, we praise Thy Name;
Lord of all, we bow before Thee!
All on earth Thy sceptre claim,
All in Heaven above adore Thee.
Infinite thy vast domain,
Everlasting is Thy reign!
Infinite Thy vast domain,
Everlasting is Thy reign!

JESUS, MY LORD, MY GOD

Jesus, my Lord, my God, my All,
How can I love Thee as I ought?
And how revere this wondrous gift,
So far surpassing hope and thought.

Sweet Sacrament we Thee adore,
O make us love Thee more and more,
O make us love Thee more and more.

Had I but Mary's sinless Heart,
To love Thee with, my dearest King,
O with what bursts of fervent praise,
Thy goodness Jesus, would I sing.

Section IV :
Holy Face Programs

AIM OF THE HOLY FACE ASSOCIATION

1. For souls to love, honour and glorify our Heavenly Father. For the glory of God is man fully alive.

2. To humbly offer reparation to the Holy Face of Jesus for the sacriliges, outrages and indifferences by which He is offended.

3. To promote vocations for the Priesthood and consecrated religious life by means of Holy Hours, as well as by personal sacrifices and acts of charity.

4. In daily thanksgiving to the Most Holy Trinity for sending Jesus who took on our humanity and who gave His Life for us by suffering and dying on the Cross.

5. To seek to console and make reparation to the Most Holy Face of Jesus and for the salvation of souls.

6. For our personal sanctification, that through the help of the Holy Face of Jesus, we shall attain eternal salvation.

7. That Our Lord's Holy Face will be known and loved by all generations, today and always.

CONDITIONS OF MEMBERSHIP

1. Wear the Holy Face medal or Holy Face scapular.

2. Enshrine the picture of the Most Holy Face of Jesus in the home and try to have it enshrined in the Church; also, if possible, start a Holy Face Holy Hour of reparation.

3. Receive the Sacrament of Reconciliation (Confession). Make a consecration of yourself and home to the Holy Face of Jesus.

4. To make the Tuesdays of reparation before the Blessed Sacrament, for a suggested period of fifteen minutes; if not possible, spend the time before the picture of the Holy Face in your home.

5. Recite prayers to the Holy Face daily or make invocation.

6. Strive to live in God's grace, which is God's Life of Love. Try to live constantly in the presence of God for we are all temples of the Holy Spirit.

7. To be faithful in assisting at ⟨
   and receiving the Sacraments, &
   the teachings of the Catholic Chur⟨

8. Try to see Christ's Face in the fa
   persons we meet each day and to bel⟨
   Jesus, the Word made Flesh.

BENEFITS AND ADVANTAGES

1. Extraordinary graces in becoming Christlike:
   faith, fortitude, overcoming all interior and
   exterior difficulties, peace, joy, gentleness,
   consolations, blessings, and dying under the
   divine gaze of Jesus Himself.

2. Assured relief of souls in Purgatory.

3. The spiritual welfare of all those known to be
   abandoned and forgotten or in need of
   salvation.

4. A personal share in all the Holy Masses, Holy
   Hours, Rosaries, Prayers and sacrifices
   performed by members of the Holy Face
   Association.

HOLY FACE CHURCH PROGRAM

If the Pastor wishes to enshrine the illuminated (or
non-illuminated), framed Holy Face picture
permanently in the church, the Association will
donate (under certain conditions) this picture plus

y Face devotional material, as well as a
rcentage of large Holy Face pictures and
venas for the parishioners. Also, the
ssociation will help to start up (preferably on
uesdays) a Holy Face Holy Hour of reparation.

HOLY FACE HOME PROGRAM
(OUR LORD COMES TO VISIT HIS CHILDREN)

A group should be formed (minimum two people;
three preferred) and they should choose a name
by which the group will be known (preferably that
of a Saint or an Angel). This designated group will
then be responsible for taking the illuminated or
non-illuminated framed Holy Face picture to
different private homes, including retirement
homes, and leave the picture at every location for
nine consecutive days. The group will recite the
first day Novena prayer with the residents of the
home and return on the ninth day to again recite
the ninth day Novena prayer, as well as the Act of
Consecration.

It is suggested that the Rosary also be said each
day in thanksgiving and reparation. After the
consecration has been made and before the
membership form is filled out, a Holy Face picture
(framed by the group) should be enshrined in the
consecrated home. The illuminated, framed Holy
Face picture is then brought to another home.

NOTE: Before starting, all in the home should be
given a Holy Face Novena, a Holy Face
explanation leaflet (with St. Theresa prayer on
the back), a promise card and a Holy Face medal
to wear before the start of the Novena. In case a
person in the home does not have a chain for the

medal, the group should always have chains, or even string if necessary. It would be nice if the group also had extra Rosaries and scapulars (brown) and explanation leaflets of both. Of course, everything we ship has been blessed by a priest. Please remember to have 12 x 16 inch Holy Face pictures on hand for the private homes. It is understood that the cost of the frame is to be paid by the group. If the group would rather have a very nice gold framed (not illuminated) Holy Face picture, they are asked to mention it, for these would be much lighter to carry.

Other available Holy Face programs include:

HOLY FACE MISSIONARY PROGRAM

HOLY FACE SCHOOL PROGRAM

HOLY FACE HOSPITAL PROGRAM

(OUR LORD CONSOLES HIS CHILDREN)

HOLY FACE PRISON PROGRAM

If you are interested in any of the programs and would like to help propagate the Devotion to the Holy Face of Jesus or become a member of the Association, please write to the address below. Distribution leaflets explaining the Devotion are available upon request in quantities of 50, 100 or 250. If you wish to adopt a church, school or other institution and become an active member of the Association, you will share in all the Masses, prayers and holy hours said by all the members.

Holy Face Association

P. O. Box 1000, Station "A"

Montreal, Quebec Canada H3C 2W9

Dear HFA,

Having the Holy Face of Jesus before me has changed my troubled life completely! I have made many novenas, but never have I come across one so powerful as that of the Holy Face of Jesus. I would like to share my miraculous discovery with my friends too, who will find consolation and help from the Holy Face of Jesus. (Mrs. F.W, USA)

Dear HFA,

I am a 10 year girl. I would like very much to wear one of these medals. Please send 6 for my family and me. This will not be forgotten in my prayers. Love, Trisha.

Dear HFA,

I have experienced real joy and blessings since I first received the pictures of the Holy face of jesus and began wearing the medal. (F.M. USA)

Dear HFA,

I want to thank you for my Holy Face medal. The pictures and the medal have brought me closer to God. I Would like to share this wonderful gift with everyone! (B.G. USA)

Dear HFA,

This medal has caused many miracles! Although it is the plainest looking of the three medals that I wear, people always notice it and even ask for it. Souls seem to be drawn to the Holy Face of Christ. Blessed be Jesus in his Passion.
(K.L. USA)

Dear HFA,

Thank you and may the good Lord bless you for the Holy Face pictures. I have already placed the lighted picture in the frame in the altar in the church. I will consecrate the whole parish to the Holy Face of our Lord and Saviour. I have already given some pictures to good people and I am also going to my neighboring parishes and my good priest friends to give them some to help spread the devotion to the Holy Face of Jesus. From the time I Started this devotion. I find many, many blessing in my parish! My heartfelt thanks, and may God bless you and your dear members of the Holy Face Association.

(Father F.P. Parish Priest)

Dear HFA,

Today, I received the pamphlet of the Holy Face of Jesus. After reading it, I felt in my heart I needed the medal. After 20 years of not going to church, I have come back to God and I realize that He never left me. So please send me the medal so that I can have Jesus close to my heart. Sincerely, K.H, (USA)

DEAR BENEFACTORS

GOD BLESS YOUR KINDNESS IN ANSWERING MY REQUEST. I'M VERY GREATFUL FOR THE MEDAL TO THE HOLY FACE WICH I WEAR AROUND MY NECK DAY AND NIGHT. I LOVE IT AND I'M SURE THAT THE DEAR FACE IS HELPING MY SPIRITUAL LIFE TO IMPROVE EVEN AFTER 62 YEARS OF RELIGIOUS LIFE. I'M TRYING TO BE A BETTER RELIGIOUS. THIS YEAR IS MY JUBILEE YEAR. I LOVE THE MEDAL, AND I AM TRYING TO DO ALL THAT THE LITERATURE TELLS US. THE HOLY CARDS ARE A DAILY REMINDER FOR ME. I WILL SHARE THEM WITH OTHERS TOO. THIS YEAR HAS BEEN VERY DIFFICULT FOR ME, BUT SOMETHING HAS HAPPENED SINCE THE ARRIVAL OF THE MEDAL. FOR 140 DAYS NOW, THE HORRENDOUS PAIN WHICH I HAD BEFORE HAS DISAPPEARED. I'M WALKING WITHOUT MY CANE AGAIN, SO RELIEVED AND JOYFUL WHILE PRAISING GOD!

(SISTER S.M., USA)

Medals Aluminium (silver or gold) of Holy Face
Medals Aluminium (silver) of Holy Face Missionary
Medals Aluminium (gold) of Holy face Missionary
Medal Metal color gold(lg,med,sm.)of Holy Face
Medal Metal color silver (lg,med,sam.) of Holy Face
Medal Metal car magnet (gold) of Holy Face
St.Dismas, St.Theresa, or St.Jude medal & prayer
Medal Aluminium (gold) St.Joseph & Virgin Mary
Positive Photo for framing (brown, 12X16)
Positive Photo for framing (black,brown, 16X20)
Positive Photo Promise Cards (brown, 4X6)
Mother Maria Pierina de Micheli Relic Card
Nine-day Novena to the Holy Face of Jesus
Holy Face Cloth Scapular
Holy Face Oil
Holy Face Chaplet
Brown Scapular
Your Key to Heaven leaflet
Your Brown Scapular leaflet
The Redeeming Power of the mass leaflet
Fifteen Promises of Mary Bookmark
Twelve Promises of the Sacred Heart Bookmark
Masses by Missionaries
Books: Life & Revelation of Saint-Gertrude
       The Holy Shroud and four Visions
       The Golden Arrow
       The Holy Man of Tours
       When Milions Saw the Shroud
       The Treasure of the Holy Face of Jesus
       Mother Marina Pierina
       I Saw the Holy Shroud

HOLY FACE ASSOCIATION
P.O. Box 1000, Station "A"
Montreal, Quebec, Canada
H3C 2W9

ORDER FORM

HOLY FACE ASSOCIATION

P.O. Box 1000, Station A, Montreal, Que. Canada H3C 2W9

Gentlemen:

Please send me_____, copies of the Treasure of the Holy Face of Jesus. Enclosed is my donation in the amount of_____.

Name_____

Street_____

City_____

State_____zip_____

Suggested Donation
           1 copy 4.00
           5 copies 3.00 each   15.00 total
          10 copies 2.50 each   25.00 total
          15 copies 2.25 each   33.75 total
          25 copies 2.00 each   50.00 total
          50 copies 1.75 each   57.50 total
         100 copies 1.50 each 150.00 total
         500 copies 1.25 each 625.00 total

‡Please include donation for packaging & postage - 10% of the value of order, minimum $2.00

The Association reserves the right to make any changes regarding the amount of the suggested donation.
subject to change without notice.

Cut Out and Mail

Why not become an apostle of the "Holy Face"? Adopt a church (with Pastor's permission) or a hospital, school, penal institution, etc., and make a promise to Our Lord and Precious Mother that you will keep that chosen place supplied with Holy Face prayer leaflets. These prayer leaflets have the "Imprimateur" accepted by the Archdiocese of Montreal – Roman Catholic Church, that souls may console the Holy Face of Jesus.

The Association, (in order to do Our Lord's Most Holy Will), does not charge for Holy Face prayer leaflets. (Postage expense would be appreciated).

☐ Yes, I (we) will help souls to love and console Jesus and would like to help spread the devotion to His Most Holy Face. Please send me (us):

☐ 50 ☐ 100 ☐ 250 prayer leaflets for distribution.

For the greater honour and glory of the Most Holy Face of Jesus, we have adopted:

Adopted: _____

Address: _____

To receive Medal, please send self-addressed, double stamped envelope to:

Holy Face Association, P.O. Box 1000, Station "A",

Montreal, Quebec, Canada H3C 2W9

(Over please)

☐ I (We) would like to place ourselves and our home under the protection of the Holy Face of Jesus (enshrine Holy Face picture in home in a place of honour) and promise to live in accordance with the teachings of the Holy Roman Catholic Church.

☐ Please enter our name as active members of the Holy Face Association recognized by the Archdiocese of Montreal.

☐ We would like to receive the Holy Face Newsletter.

Name: _____ Date: _____

Address: _____

City, State: _____ Zip: _____

I wish to help with a donation of: _____

Income tax receipt will be sent for donations of $20.00 (Canadian) or more. Thank you.